30 WAYS A MOTHER CAN BLESS HER CHILDREN

JOHN TRENT, PH.D.

30 Ways a Mother Can Bless Her Children

Aspire Press, an imprint of Rose Publishing, LLC
P.O. Box 3473
Peabody, Massachusetts 01961-3473 USA
Email: info@hendricksonrose.com
www.hendricksonrose.com

Special thanks to Kari Trent and Tamara Love for their assistance in making these books possible.

Printed in the United States of America
December 2017, 2nd printing

THE POWER OF A MOTHER'S BLESSING

MY TWIN BROTHER and I were only two months old when our father left. I didn't hear the shock in my mother's voice when she picked up the phone, and he told her that the reason his clothes were gone was because he was not only moving out but also moving on. I didn't hear her cry. I didn't understand the despair she felt as a suddenly single parent with no job, no college degree, no money, no help from her family, and (in that day) no help from the government.

In 1952 when my mother got that wake-up call, the divorce rate was four couples per thousand. No, that's not a typo. *Four couples per thousand.*

Suddenly she was not only a minority but also a minority that was looked down upon by the vast majority of society.

So she went to business school and became a career woman in the early '50s, a pioneer by circumstances, not by choice. She was the thirteenth employee at First Federal Savings and Loan and ascended to the level of first vice president at an amazing clip. The *only* vice president in the firm who was a woman. She was so accomplished that in 1956, a pen-and-ink drawing of my mother was on the front cover of the *Wall Street Journal*, which did a profile on her! But that's not what I remember about her as a child. What I remember most were the hundreds of ways she blessed us.

WHAT I REMEMBER MOST WERE THE HUNDREDS OF WAYS SHE BLESSED US.

I'll share with you soon just one way she blessed

me. Then I'll share with you thirty more ways—you-can-do-this! ways—of creating a legacy of love in the life of each child God's placed in your care. What I share are ways that I saw my mother use with us boys (along with my twin, I had an older brother), ways that I watched the tremendous mother of our two daughters (my wife, Cindy) use to bless our girls, and ways other extraordinary mothers shared with me of how they blessed their children.

WHAT THE BLESSING IS

In the Old Testament, we are introduced to the practice of parents passing on a blessing to their children. A well-known biblical account of the giving of the blessing is found in the Genesis story of Jacob and Esau. (Look up Genesis 27 if you'd like to read it yourself.)

Jacob and Esau were fraternal twin sons of Isaac. All their lives, each son sought after his father's blessing. But in this home, only one son would receive the blessing, and the other would cry out when he found he had missed it forever, "Bless me, even me also, O my father!" (Genesis 27:34).

That same thing, I'm convinced, takes place in every home today.

In every home, with every mother, there is a choice set: a choice to bless her children—to communicate that incredible gift of unconditional love and acceptance that her children long for from the earliest years forward—or to actively or passively withhold the blessing from her children, leading to a lifetime of emotional hurt.

The words may be different from Esau's terrible cry in the Bible—"Do you have only one blessing, my father? Bless me, even me also, O my father" (Genesis 27:38)—but I hear those kinds of heartbreaking words echoed in my counseling office week after week from a now-grown son or daughter, someone who still longs for that gift that was never given, that blessing that never came from their mother.

And that's so wrong and unnecessary! There are so many times I wish I could turn back the years and sit down with that mother who's chosen to withhold the blessing, to share with her why it's so important and explain why God blessed us and how we can, in turn, bless others, starting with our own family. And in most cases, what I'd likely find out is that she just didn't know! She just simply didn't know how important it was to bless her children—and too often, that's because she never got the blessing herself!

If you did get the blessing growing up as a child, then you'll get the concepts that follow right away. You lived them. They'll remind you of the many similar ideas you experienced up close and personal from your own mother as you got the blessing. They'll motivate you to do what you've experienced. If you didn't get the blessing growing up, this book is crucial for you. You need to know that water can rise above its own level. You can reverse the curse, even if it's generations long. You can learn what it means to bless others. You'll see how in so many small ways, you can hand that incredible gift of the blessing to your kids (and your spouse) and experience it yourself!

WHY CHOOSE TO BLESS

Life over Death, Blessing over Curse

In Deuteronomy, the Lord says to his people, "I call heaven and earth to witness against you today, that I have set before you life and death, blessing and curse. Therefore choose life, that you and your offspring may live" (Deuteronomy 30:19, ESV). That's one choice with two parts: (1) life over death, and (2) blessing over curse. In Scripture the word *life* means movement; things that are alive are moving towards someone or something. The word *death* means to step away. That's a word picture of your first choice as a mother.

Are you going to step towards your children—with appropriate touch, with spoken words that attach high value, by picturing a special future for them and showing them your genuine commitment? Or are you going to choose to step away—because of work, because you just don't know how to bless them, or because you never got the blessing yourself?

EVEN IF WE OURSELVES NEVER GOT THE BLESSING GROWING UP, WE CAN CHANGE THE PICTURES OF OUR LIFE STORY!

There is no middle ground. Your children will look back on your relationship with them when they've grown up, and they will know in their heart of hearts the answer to this question: *Did my mother choose to step towards me or away from me?* No mother is perfect. But each mother has that choice set before her: to choose life over death, to step towards or to step away.

And know this: what keeps us choosing to step towards our children (and our spouse) is having made that first foundational choice for life in Christ! That's LIFE in all capitals!

The new life Jesus gives us when we choose him gets us moving towards others in service, love, and commitment! The abundant life he offers us gives us his power and strength to keep moving towards our children in a positive way—even on those days (or seasons) when it's tough or difficult to do so or when we really feel like stepping away. Even if we ourselves never got the blessing growing up, we can change the pictures of our life story! Jesus promised us, "I have come that you might have life, and have it abundantly" (John 10:10). He gets us unstuck and moving towards him—and towards others!

So that's the choice set before you. Are you going to step towards or step away from the Lord? To step towards or away from your children? Your spouse?

Very soon, you'll learn thirty ways mothers have stepped towards their children, ways that I've taught to mothers across the planet to bless their children as well. They're not the only thirty that count. You can adjust and even change every one. But you'll soon see that it's small things like these examples that you can draw on to communicate God's love to your children. In small but often unforgettable ways, you can say to them "I'm crazy about you" as you get moving towards your children. Amazingly, those small things over time create what we call a culture of the blessing in your home.

Two Word Pictures

In Scripture, the Hebrew word for *to bless* suggests two pictures. The first picture is that of bowing the knee. This doesn't mean we have to bow literally to our children! That would be a little strange and confusing to them in our culture! But it's a picture of our acknowledging–which bowing did in olden times and still does in some cultures–that we are in the presence of someone who's extremely valuable. In this case, it's our children who we've chosen to bless.

The second picture of blessing carries the idea of adding weight or value–like adding coins to an ancient scale. The greater the weight, the higher the value. Our actions towards our children should say, "You are valuable to me, and I choose to add to your life."

Think about how we bless the Lord. When we say that (or sing those words), we're really saying,

"Lord, you're so valuable, I bow the knee before you." But then we add our praise to him. In short, when we bless a child, we're acknowledging in our heart that our child has great worth and value, and then we act on that choice to value them by adding to their life!

A Culture of Blessing

But what do we add to bless a child (or others)? As a mother, you'll see there are five things, or elements, of the blessing that surface every time the blessing was given in Scripture (more details about these shortly). Amazingly, while God's Word was written centuries ago, those same five elements of the blessing are foundational in clinical research reflecting what makes healthy families!

YOU CAN PASS ON THE BLESSING TO YOUR CHILDREN IN SMALL WAYS EVERY DAY AS WELL.

Of course, the act of a mother's giving of the blessing isn't just reserved for a once-in-a-lifetime momentous occasion. There were times in Scripture when the blessing was given at the end of a parent's life, but you see other times when very young children were given the blessing! Jesus blessed young children that weren't his own. In fact, a father or mother in biblical times could bless their children *every day*. And you can pass on the blessing to your children in small ways every day as well.

PUT THAT DEEP-SEATED KNOWLEDGE OF UNCONDITIONAL ACCEPTANCE IN YOUR CHILD'S HEART

In fact, it's all these small, specific, positive ways that can help you as a mother create what we call a culture of the blessing in your home! Think about a culture like setting a thermostat in your home. Try living in Chicago in February and setting the thermostat at 20 degrees throughout the house. No matter where you go in that home, the atmosphere, or culture, communicates one thing: it's cold! Your whole focus isn't on relating to others or being free to do things inside; your focus is on getting warm!

But now set the thermostat at 72 degrees and watch life warm up and the focus of your family go from what's missing (heat) to all the things you *can do* as a family! You've added life (movement) to the home, because you've changed the thermostat (or culture)! And when you create a culture of the blessing in the home, kids grow up knowing "I've got it! I've got my parent's blessing!" No searching for it all their life like too many children are forced to do. No focus on what's lost but on freedom to move towards God's best!

Here's an example from my own home to illustrate.

When Kari, our oldest child, was about five years old, we'd done many of the thirty things you'll see in this book to build into her life the blessing. But one night, she had "one of those nights" when it was really hard for her to go to sleep. We brought her water. Then a second glass of water, this time with ice cubes. Then there was the trip to the bathroom after all that water. Then a warm washcloth to soothe her. But at that point, it was obvious this was just becoming a game. That's when I told her, "That's it, Kari. No more getting out of bed. Period. We'll see you in the morning."

Kari didn't get out of bed again. But she did something that my wife and I have never forgotten: from down the hall, Kari yelled out to us, "'Night, Mom! 'Night, Dad! And don't forget to bless me in the morning!"

Cindy and I just looked at each other and the feelings were overwhelming. Neither Cindy nor I grew up in a home where we had that kind of certainty and love and blessing. Cindy came from an alcoholic home, and I came from a single-parent home. And neither one of us had grown up in a Christian home. Yet here was Kari (finally) heading off to sleep, reminding us to have that gift waiting for her in the morning. Not a Christmas or birthday present. Something even more important to a child. She knew she had our blessing.

And this book can help you put that kind of unconditional love—that kind of "I got it!" deep-seated knowledge of unconditional acceptance—in the center of your son and daughter's heart. Something that can impact their life today and can point them towards God's best and his blessing tomorrow.

BLESSING BASICS

The Five Essential Elements

Let's get more specific about just what we mean by the blessing, before we jump into the thirty you-can-do-this! examples coming up. The reason why is you'll see them pop up in the suggestions and examples that follow.

First, the blessing begins with a meaningful touch. The blessing continues with a spoken message, meaning you say or write out your blessing, so it was unmistakable. The third element of the blessing is how your words always express high value. Fourth, you imagine a special future for your child. And then these four attitudes and actions are lived out and demonstrated through an active commitment to see the blessing come to pass in your child's life.

Each of these five elements contributes its own impact on your blessing.

Meaningful Touch

A *meaningful touch* was an important part of giving the blessing in the Old Testament. When Isaac blessed his son, he called him, saying, "Come near and kiss me, my son" (Genesis 27:26, ESV). Isaac's words "come near" actually translate as "come and embrace in a bear hug." Isaac believed he was speaking to Esau, who was more than forty years old at the time! Isaac sets an example of a parent who didn't limit touch to his children due to their age, an example mothers (and fathers) should pay attention to. The benefits of touch are enormous—physically, emotionally, and spiritually.

Spoken Message

A *spoken message* has the power to build up or tear down a child's worth and heart and are a big part of cementing your love and building a healthy attachment to your children. Can you remember words of praise that your mother spoke to you? What about words of criticism? Our words hold great power, and the blessing acknowledges this through the spoken message. In the Bible, a blessing was invalid unless it was spoken. In the book of James, we see multiple pictures of the power of the tongue. The tongue is described as a bit that gives direction to a horse, a rudder that turns a ship, and a spreading fire (James 3:1–6). Each of these pictures shows us the potential of the tongue to build up or tear down. Will your tongue be one that encourages or belittles? Children desperately need to hear positive words spoken to them. The words of a mother hold incredible weight in the heart of a child. Choose to speak words of blessing to your children.

CHOOSE TO SPEAK WORDS OF BLESSING TO YOUR CHILDREN.

High Value

But what kind of words are we to speak or write down for our children? Those that communicate *high value*. To value something is to attach great importance to it. In blessing our children, we are choosing to ascribe great worth to them, acknowledging that they are valuable to the Lord and to us. This is important, even in times of difficulty with our children. Children push our buttons, try us emotionally, exhaust us physically, and often deplete us financially! But in the times when we may not feel the value of our children, choosing to speak words of high value to them realigns our own perspective and encourages our children to see their value as well.

RULES WITHOUT A RELATIONSHIP IS A GREAT WAY TO BREED REBELLION IN A CHILD'S HEART.

Special Future

With our *meaningful touch*, with our choice to use a *spoken message*, and by attaching words with *high value* to a child, we lay the foundation to help us picture a *special future* for our children as well. As we attach value to a person, we can see their potential and envision the great ways in which they might impact the world for Christ. Kids are literalists when it comes to hearing words that point them towards a special future or when they hear that they're a failure, pathetic, or a loser. By paying attention to the strengths your child exhibits, you can see how that sensitivity they show with other children today might make them a great counselor, teacher, or coach down the road; how that leadership talent today could be something that Jesus uses to help them change the world for the better tomorrow. Every person is gifted uniquely. How are your children gifted? How might their strengths benefit their relationships and future endeavors? Paint a picture with your words of your children's future and it can be, literally, unforgettable for them as they go through life.

Active Commitment

The last element of the blessing really seals the deal, as the one giving the blessing demonstrates an *active commitment* to see the blessing come to pass in that child's life. Words have to be accompanied by action. The blessing is not merely spoken but lived—even when it's hard. Giving the blessing to your children doesn't mean you don't discipline them. All kids are like you. Fallen. In need of a Savior. And in need of someone who loves them enough to say no at times, to point them down the right path, and to correct wrongs. But rules without a relationship is a great way to breed rebellion in a child's heart. The blessing gives you the platform to do discipline well, because your children know you love them deeply and care what direction their life is taking.

Mom, be intentional about connecting with and blessing your children today. And as you do, you will be adding layer after layer of love and acceptance into their life that they'll need and can draw strength from all their lives!

And you're not alone in doing this! The Lord honors those who seek him and depend on him for help. We're to be the spiritual trainers in our home (Deuteronomy 6:6–9). And we serve a great and mighty God who can keep us stepping towards our children, not stepping away.

Here's a way to remember all the various elements that make up the blessing—a way I teach to people, through an acronym: BLESS. While the elements are rearranged in order from our discussion, using this acronym is an easy way to remember all five elements.

B stands for "be committed" (active commitment)

L stands for "lovingly touch" (meaningful touch)

E stands for "express value" (high value)

S stands for "see potential" (special future)

S stands for "say it!" (spoken message)

You might consider posting this acronym on your fridge, on your bathroom mirror, or maybe by your desk computer—somewhere that you look regularly and can be reminded of your own desire to give the blessing to your son or daughter. Use it as a tool to check up on yourself and evaluate how you are doing with each element.

Show-and-Tell

So now you know what the blessing is, why it's so important to choose to bless your children's life, and what the basics are. The rest of the book is show-and-tell.

Any teacher knows that show-and-tell can be even more powerful than just tell. So in the pages that follow, I want to show you simple, practical ways that mothers have used to pass on the blessing to a child.

You certainly aren't limited to these, but I hope they will act as a springboard for your efforts to pass on the blessing to your children. You will see that each suggestion incorporates a variety of the five elements of the blessing. Some focus on using spoken words. Others incorporate a meaningful touch or help you to picture a special future. In some of the examples and occasions discussed, you'll see where all five come together in one activity or suggestion! And, yes, some aspects of each blessing might be easier for you to give than others. But the cumulative result of implementing all five elements of the blessing will help your children in so many ways—emotionally, physically, spiritually.

Moms are the busiest people on the planet! I'm not asking you to try to force your way, by sheer willpower, to bless your children. Rather, in freedom and drawing on your faith, start by just reading these ideas. Even just the first one. Then start adapting them in your own home. Try them out. Make up your own. Remember a way you were blessed, and pass that on to your children and speak it into their life.

You goal isn't to try and mark a checklist as you use each example. Every attempt at passing on the blessing doesn't have to meet a list of must-do criteria. And there's no need to do each one perfectly. Nor does passing on a blessing have to result in the best evening ever or some huge emotional response from your child: "Oh, thanks, Mom, for spending time with me. I'll remember this all my life."

What you're looking to do is choose to layer in the blessing—to create that 72-degree culture of caring, acceptance, commitment, and courage in your home. It's not about perfection or emotion or doing something just right. It is about jumping in and going all in on being a mother who is going to *choose* to bless her children.

YOUR WORDS AND ACTIONS CAN SAY, "I'M CRAZY ABOUT YOU!"

And guess what will happen over time.

Over time, by choosing to bless your children—even a challenging child and even on days when it's not so easy to do so—you'll start creating that culture of the blessing in your home. You'll see the blessing become a habit that enriches your family and eats discouragement and bad attitudes.

As you read these examples, they may bring back a memory of a time or way your own mother gave you her blessing—with her spoken or written words, by a gentle touch, by attaching high value to you, by picturing a special future for you, and by living out a life of genuine commitment. Perhaps after you've read these, you'll pick a few that remind you of her. If she's living and was a blessing to you, take time to call her and tell her what a blessing she was to you, and then get ready to bless your own family.

But even if you didn't get the blessing in your home growing up, *you can turn things around in your life and family!* Your words and actions can attach high value to your children and say to them, "I'm crazy about you!"

Trust me: every child, in every home, deserves to have someone who's crazy about them! Beyond that, every child in every home deserves to know that *Jesus* is crazy about them as well. They need someone who communicates this "I'm all in" about you, someone who has chosen to bless them. It can change a child's life today and point them towards a special future tomorrow.

So let me share with you one way my own mother blessed me that is within your power to do with your children. In fact, it's right there at the tip of your fingers. And then be encouraged and enjoy diving into idea after idea of ways to bless your children!

A MOTHER'S HANDS—ONE WAY TO BLESS

I SHARED EARLIER that my mother was an incredible businesswoman. But she was even better at giving her three sons her blessing. And one way she did that was with her hands.

When I think of my childhood, my thoughts range over a thousand pictures of my mother's hands. By the time I was ten, my mother's business career was over, due to crippling, debilitating rheumatoid arthritis that twisted her hands and bent her wrists. But while the arthritis took away her career, it didn't touch her ability to bless us, even with those twisted, beautiful hands.

Because of the pain in her twisted joints, my mother could not grab anyone's hand. She never took a person's hand and shook it. When she took a person's hand, she touched it gently, squeezing just a part of it, holding on softly and then releasing it from her touch. She held everything loosely—cups, silverware, pencils. She even held the days loosely, never knowing whether it would be a good day or a bad one, yet taking whatever came and taking it with grace.

> LITTLE BY LITTLE, THE WARMTH OF HER HANDS AND HEART MELTED OURS HEARTS.

That's how she held on to each of us boys as we grew up: tenderly, softly, with great affection and warmth.

Because her hands hurt her so much, my mother was never able to spank us, but beneath her tender ways there was an underlying firmness. Worse than a spanking was her way of placing her hands on ours, always softly, and speaking to us, always gently, of her concern about our behavior. When she looked up at one of us and held our hand, we might as well have been in the grip of a lumberjack. We couldn't pull away. It would hurt her hands if we did.

So we sat there.

And we listened.

And little by little, the warmth of her hands and heart melted ours.

Whatever I lost in a dad, I gained in a mom. She was the compensating grace in my life. She couldn't do much with her hands in the way of ironing slacks or sewing on buttons or even cooking a meal. But with her hands—her meaningful touch—she communicated so much to us. One picture at a time. One blessing at a time.

Do you know that Michelangelo believed that the hardest feature to capture in his sculptures were his subject's *hands*? That's because hands are so unique and because they carry so much of a person's character.

What pictures do you have of your mother's hands blessing you?

- Perhaps you see your mother's hands folding a damp washcloth and laying it gently on your fevered forehead.
- Perhaps you see your mother clapping her hands for you when you scored a goal or finished a dance recital.
- Perhaps you see your mother's hands typing that term paper late at night to help you pass a class.
- Maybe you see your mother waving to you at graduation.
- Maybe you see your mother's hands folded in prayer for you during that time of your deepest hurt.

These are only a few ways a mother can bless her child with her hands.

You can use your hands to bless and encourage your children in so many ways. But don't stop there. Jump in now and start reading about thirty different ways you can give and live the blessing.

30 WAYS TO BLESS YOUR CHILDREN

Read-Aloud Blessing

One way my wife, Cindy, used to bless our girls was by taking time to read with them. While we did the traditional bedtime stories, Cindy also found several additional ways to make reading with our girls something that gave them her blessing and created a bond between all of us. I'm happy to say that even though our girls are grown, this tradition can still be found on Trent family road trips and when our girls are home for holidays. Here are some ways to turn a bedtime story or time in the car into a time of blessing for your child:

- Change your child's name to the name of a hero or heroine of the book you are reading. As Cindy read through *The Chronicles of Narnia*, she changed Princess Lucy's name to Princess Kari (the name of our oldest daughter). This showed Kari that she was Cindy's heroine and that she would pick her over Lucy any day of the week. With this simple change, Kari couldn't wait for bedtime, and these are still some of her favorite books today.

- While reading, take moments to pause to bless your child. Often Cindy would do this by calling attention to positive character traits happening in the story. For example, if a character in the story shares a toy, pause and tell your child that they are also really good at sharing. I'd encourage you to go beyond a compliment and make it something that sticks with them. To do this, give an example of when you saw them exhibiting the specific trait. To use the sharing example above, instead of saying "Timmy, you are good at sharing." You could say, "Timmy, this reminds me of you. I saw how you let your little brother play with a toy you really wanted today. I'm so proud of you for sharing, and I love the way you look out for your little brother." This can become a great way to specifically point out great things your child does in a way that will continue to stick with and encourage them.

- Pick a book series to read together whenever you are in the car (if you get carsick, pick an audio book to listen to together). Our youngest daughter, Laura, and I would read every time we were in the car together. We did this from the time she was five all the way until I was driving her from Arizona to Texas for college. This time of bonding gave us time to talk between chapters and allowed me to bless Laura by spending quality time with her in an interactive way. Plus there were always positive things in her that I could point out to her as she read.

Reading is a great way to make blessing your children a part of your daily routine. That's the key to your children knowing that they have your blessing. It's not just a one-time event—it's a daily affirmation of who they are and the special future that God has for them. Remember that Scripture says: "Encourage one another and build one another up, just as you are doing (1 Thessalonians 5:11, ESV).

Board of Blessing

Teach your kids the importance of calling attention to positive traits in others by creating a place for all members of the family to anonymously post encouragement to one another.

For example, if your son notices his sister sharing a toy that she is especially attached to, he can write "Great job sharing your slinky!" on the board. (If your kids don't know how to write, they can draw a picture or ask you to write for them.) Make sure you have spots on the board for Mom and Dad as well!

Every night before your children go to bed, you can read the notes of encouragement together as a family. As you begin this habit, you'll want to pave the way by making an effort to write something to each family member every day for a week or so. This creates a practice of seeing the best in each other on a daily basis and gives a space for those things to be celebrated and called out. This also allows for blessing to become a habit and take a place of importance in your family relationships. It's a simple way to teach your son or daughter to look for the strengths of those around them and gives them tools to point those strengths out.

As added incentive in our home, when one of our children received ten nice notes in a row, they would get to pick out a movie for the family to watch or get to choose a special candy treat to celebrate. You could consider doing something similar.

Teaching your children at a young age to bless others will translate into a habit of blessing others as they get older.

3

Practice-Hospitality Blessing

One of our favorite traditions as a family happens on holidays. No matter what the holiday is, we all reach out to people in our lives who don't have family in the area, and we invite them to come spend the holiday with us.

I know that the concept of Friendsgiving (Thanksgiving with friends instead of family) is a popular one, but for the past twenty-five years, we have used this model for every holiday—Christmas Day, Fourth of July, Martin Luther King Jr. Day, Easter—you name it.

We still keep quality time as a family, but we all get excited as new friends come over, and it's been fun to watch as deep connections were built over the years.

One family in particular has been spending holidays with us for over twenty-five years, and our kids have deep friendships with one another. Now our kids are all living out this culture of blessing by carrying on this tradition as they build their own families in different places across the country.

Making your home a place of blessing for others is just one way that you can bless your kids and teach them to pass that blessing onto others. Here are some other ideas to practice hospitality and help create a culture of blessing in your home:

- Help your kids make a welcome sign or card for guests who are coming over.
- Invite friends who don't have family in the area to come celebrate a holiday with your family. We would spend Christmas Eve and Christmas morning as a family. Then we would invite others over around noon for a lunch, and then we'd end the day with everyone going to a movie. As our kids got older, they would even have game nights at our house after the movie. This would give us time as a family, as well as make our home

a place of blessing for others on days that can be really lonely for people without family.

- Help your kids brainstorm fun ideas for gifts to bless the people who come to the house. You can do this for people your family goes to visit as well. You can put all the suggestions—which can be as simple as make a drawing or write a note—in a jar and pick one out to do before your guest(s) arrive.

- Teach your kids to look for those who may need a friend. Encouraging your kids to invite over the kid who was made fun of in class or the one who may not have someone to eat lunch with may do more to bless them than you can imagine.

4

Post-It®-Note Blessing

Every year on Parent Night at our girls' elementary school, Cindy and I would take time to bless our girls. While the teacher showed us the classroom, Cindy and I would take sticky notes and hide them in various places where our girls would later be able find them: under their desk, on top of the desk, inside a textbook, in their cubby, inside their pencil box, on the seat of their chair–you name it.

Each of these sticky notes had a note of encouragement for our girls to find throughout the year. We prayed over the notes as we hid them, and we prayed that in moments when our daughters really needed encouragement–or needed to know that they had value–a note would be found.

Each year the girls looked forward to showing up at school after Parent Night and finding visible reminders of how much Cindy and I loved them.

Here are some other fun ways to use sticky notes to bless your sons and daughters throughout the year:

- Put a sticky note on their bedroom door after they're asleep, so when they wake up in the morning, they are reminded of how loved and valued they are.
- Put a sticky note on a school paper or test that they didn't do well on. Encourage them that this paper or test doesn't define them and that they are going to rock the next one.
- Put a sticky note of encouragement inside their lunch box.
- When they go stay with the grandparents or spend the night at a friend's house, hide a blessing sticky note in their overnight bag.
- Put an encouraging "I'm proud of you" sticky note on a project they worked particularly hard on.

Giving the blessing to your sons and daughters is something that will stick with them, just like the simple little notes stuck in everyday places. Remember these words from Proverbs: "Gracious words are like a honeycomb, sweetness to the soul and health to the body" (Proverbs 16:24, ESV).

5

Give-Stuff-Away Blessing

We live in a highly materialistic society where it is exceedingly easy to accumulate more and more and more stuff. There is something to be said about pursuing simplicity and teaching our kids contentment. One way to do this is to teach our kids to give stuff away. Here are just a few creative ways to do this with your own children:

- As a family, clean out your rooms. Explain to your children beforehand that everything they give away will go to a local shelter to help kids who don't have anything. Take

One of our family's favorite things to do when our girls were young was to make brownies. This time spent together involved a lot of broken eggshells in the mix, overpouring of vegetable oil, and even more laughter.

Once, when Cindy was out of town, we even turned our brownie mix into chocolate face painting. I'm not exactly sure how it started, but by the end of it, all three of us (and our kitchen) were covered in chocolate and crying from laughing so hard. We painted designs on each others faces and afterwards jumped in the pool to clean up the mess.

While Cindy established some guidelines for Chocolate Face Painting after that (mainly, clean up the kitchen and use the hose instead of the pool), i became one our favorite activities.

Those times spent together in the kitchen shc our girls that they could make mistakes and st' d up with something delicious. It showed them we were proud of them, even if the brownies d up burnt because there was more mix on us in the baking pan. And it gave us a time to be and have fun and build memories that would ' a lifetime.

While chocolate face painting may not be for you, there are plenty of other ways to make meal prep a time of blessing instead of chaos:

- Teach your kids to make an easy dessert. Let them be in charge of that dessert and serve it to the family at dinner.
- For younger kids, pick a meal that has no more than three ingredients and let them make dinner (with help, as needed).
- Let older kids pick a meal of their choice and cook it with them. You can even include a trip to the grocery store where they can purchase the ingredients they will need.
- Do your own version of Chocolate Face Painting. I'd recommend wearing clothes that can be trashed, doing it on an outside patio, or even turning it into a food fight in the backyard.
- Give daily mealtime tasks. No kid loves to set the table, but having a dinner prep job can make cooking a time of blessing. Give your

kids several options of ways they can help with the meal, and let them take ownership of the task they choose. Affirm them as they finish what they started.

Making time in the kitchen an intentional time of blessing can change the atmosphere of your home. I totally understand that allowing your children to participate can slow things down, but by making them a part of the process, they will gain confidence in more than just their cooking skills. They will gain confidence in the fact that they have your blessing.

Special-Plate Blessing

Our family loves to celebrate. Everything from passing a test one of our girls was worried about to making the varsity cheer squad was given attention and affirmation from each member of the family.

One of our favorite ways of celebrating was to use the Special Plate at dinner. Each of our girls had picked out her own Special Plate, and when something exciting happened in their lives, they would get to use that at dinner while the rest of the family celebrated with them but used the regular dinnerware. It was like getting to have a mini-party each and every time they were excited about something.

This simple way of celebrating even little accomplishments showed our girls that we were right there with them. We were excited for them, proud of them, and truly cared about the little things going on in their lives. It created a fun and safe place to talk about the ups and downs of the day, and our girls knew that they had a team of cheerleaders behind them no matter what.

In our family, we could also nominate a family member who had done something that deserved the Special Plate. This helped our girls to learn to "rejoice with those who rejoice," even when the spotlight wasn't on them (Romans 12:15). It showed them that putting the spotlight on others often felt even better than receiving it themselves. It's important for children to feel celebrated, but it's equally important for them to learn to celebrate the successes of others.

You could have your kids pick out a Special Plate at the store, or you could go to a ceramics shop and have each family member create their own Special Plate to celebrate small achievements. This would allow for a fun family memory for everyone each time the Special Plates are used.

The great part is, the type of food on the plate isn't important. Even if you're eating leftovers, takeout, or a PB&J sandwich on the Special Plate, using the plate is a simple, fun, and affirming way to celebrate life's little moments with your child. Remember: "Everyone should eat and drink and take pleasure in all his toil—this is God's gift to man" (Ecclesiastes 3:13, ESV).

9

Special-Display Blessing

Our daughters, Kari and Laura, used to love coming to my office. Aside from the fact that I had a secret stash of candy hidden in my desk, they also loved seeing their artwork, stories, and craft creations on display for the world to see.

I would continually rotate in their newest creation on my desk and even had a few proudly displayed in our lobby. They'd walk in and immediately know that I was proud of them and that they had my blessing.

My precious awesome wife, Cindy, did the same thing in our home. She would proudly display what the girls made on the refrigerator as well as on a Pinterest-worthy bulletin board. Every time they would come in the house or go into the kitchen, they would be reminded that she thought they had talent and value.

There are also other ways that you can display your children's work:

- Take pictures of what they've created, and turn it into your desktop background or screen saver.

- Post a photo of an especially good school report or drawing on social media, blessing your child in such a way that everyone on social media can see (make sure you let them see the post and any encouraging comments from friends and family members).

- Have a family art show where your kids are able to hang up a variety of creations and grandma, grandpa, you, and any other special family members are invited to attend. You can even have your child designate specific pieces of art to go home with each of your guests.

- If your children love to dance or sing, let them put on a concert for you. Some of our favorite family home videos are of our girls tap dancing to their own musical creation.

Make sure you get the performance on video so they can watch it; and praise them for their boldness and innovation!

- If your children love to write, schedule time for them to read what they are working on with you. You can even frame a poem or short story that they write and find a special place to display it, like on a wall or on your bookshelf.
- Frame a drawing or painting they make and put it on your desk or nightstand.

No matter what form your children's creation takes, the important thing is that your kids should get a visual reminder that they have value to you. They pour their hearts into creating, imagining, and inventing. Letting them know that they have your blessing to pursue those creative outlets fosters trust as they move onto bigger areas of life. Celebrating the small successes gives permission to be a part of the big ones.

Snail-Mail Blessing

In today's world of email and text messages, the use of snail mail for the delivery of messages has been significantly reduced. But receiving a letter in the mail shows that a person took the time to personally handwrite a message, address an envelope, stick on a stamp (after they track one down), and get it into the mailbox. Honestly, making it through all of those steps is rare anymore! That's why one amazing way to bless your children is to write and mail them a letter.

Write them a letter of encouragement. Do they have a big test coming up? Are they having trouble with friends at school? Is math class feeling like an impossible mountain for them to climb? Take time to write a few lines to tell them you love them, you are proud of them, and no matter what they are up against, you have their back—and so does the Lord.

You can include verses, a picture, or anything else that you feel would encourage them.

Mail the letter from a public mailbox, and surprise them when it arrives by letting them get it from the mailbox.

If you do this for big and small occasions, every five minutes you spend writing can create a lifetime of written blessings for your child to read whenever things get challenging as they grow.

Cindy and I continued to do this as our girls headed to college. Once a week we'd buy a card, write a note of encouragement to them, and send it to their college mailbox. Our girls still have a stockpile of these cards (and even have some hanging in their room) for encouragement and as reminders of our blessing in moments when life has challenges.

Here are some other ideas to help bless your kids by writing to them:

- If you are traveling for work or even vacationing away from your kids, buy a postcard from the city you are in and write a note of blessing to them. It will make their day when it arrives at home!

- Buy a pack of silly cards and mail one a month with a note of encouragement or a blessing about something specific going on in their life. It can be funny or serious.
- If your kid goes to camp for the summer, write them a letter for each day that they are gone and put them in their luggage.

There is something so powerful about your written affirmation that sticks with your kids. I guarantee the five minutes (or less) that it takes you to write them a note will be more than worth the smile on their face as they get real mail, open your card, and receive your blessing.

Selfie Blessing

Don't underestimate the power of a selfie when it comes to blessing your kids. In today's world of smartphones, it's never been easier to give your kid your blessing. Taking a picture together not only gives them a moment of your full attention, but it also communicates to them that they are just as valuable as your friends, the pretty cup of coffee that you got, or the duck that flew into your pool.

Here are several ways for you to turn selfies into blessings for your kids:

- Have a selfie photo shoot with your son or daughter the next time you are out together.
- When you are putting your kids to bed, turn off the lights, sit on the bed with them, and turn your camera to selfie mode. Make sure that the flash is on. Count to three and

each of you make a silly face. Then snap the picture. Repeat this several times, each time making a different silly face. Once you have several photos taken, look at the pictures together and enjoy a few moments of rich laughter over the silly faces that you made. Laughing with your kids is one of the best ways to tear down walls and share memories of blessing with them.

- Have a selfie competition. Take turns snapping silly selfies together when you are running errands with your kids. When you get home, vote on your favorite selfie, and make it the family computer desktop background for the week.

- For older kids, designate a Saturday as Selfie Saturday and have a family text chat that day. Have each family member submit silly selfies as they go through their day. This is a great way for your family to stay connected, even when your kids go to high school or off to college. At the end of the day, vote as a family on the winning selfie. The losers have to set the winning image as their phone background for the rest of the week.

- For your son or daughter's birthday, print off your favorite selfie with them and put it in a frame. Giving your kids an actual picture of your blessing and love for them will help remind them that even on days when things aren't sunny, they can come back to the truth that you love them and are there for them.

A picture really is worth a thousand words. Any way that you can show your kids physical pictures of how much you care about them blesses them beyond measure. Even something as simple as setting your phone's background to a picture of your family reminds them each time they see it that they have your blessing. They are wanted. They are a priority. And they have great value to you.

In other words, they matter—more than anything else you could take a picture of.

12

Part-of-the-Family Blessing

We had a rule in our house growing up: once a friend had been to our home three times, they were officially considered one of the family.

While our kids at the time thought that we were allowing people to be a part of our family so that we no longer had to offer them a drink when they came in (as family, they could get their own) or a snack (they could go in the fridge and get string cheese and an apple or whatever other snack Cindy had ready for them), for Cindy and I, there were several strategic reasons we invited the kids coming to our house to be a part of our family:

- We realized that if a kid came to our house three times or more, they were reaching close-friend status in our kids' lives. This meant that this was someone they were spending a good amount of time with at school or on the sports team. This was more than just an acquaintance.

- We wanted to make sure that we got to know the friends our kids were hanging around with. If they came over regularly, we knew that we had the chance to get to know them. By inviting them to be part of the family, we created a nonthreatening, welcoming atmosphere for them to be a part of.

- This created a level of acceptance in our home that led to real conversations, instead of polite but fake conversations. Again, the goal was to get to know the kids that our kids were spending time with.

- We noticed that there were a few kids who came into our home who didn't have what I would call a real family. Sure, they had parents, but they never had dinners with them, didn't have adults to process life with, and didn't have anyone who would show up to their games or cheer them up after a rough day at school. By inviting them into our family, they had a safe place to go through the ups and downs of being a kid, as well as the opportunity to see what being a part of a family looked like.

When I was in high school, there was a family that "adopted" me. I would watch them cook dinner together and eat together as a family, and I'd see the parents tuck their kids in at night. They displayed a love for each other and for the Lord that I had never experienced before. That love in their home showed me that loving Jesus made all the difference. Cindy and I wanted the kids in our home to experience that same sort of blessing.

When our kids' friends reached the third-visit stage, we would invite them to stay for dinner, give them a Special Plate, and verbally give them our blessing and welcome them into our family. There were a lot of laughs about how they would now have to do chores (which typically meant walking the dogs or helping us clean up after dinner). But there was also in our home an invitation offered to them to be free to be who God created them to be. In a casual, fun way, we wanted them to know that they could be themselves, and we wanted to show them that they had value and acceptance to us the second they walked in the door.

Welcoming your kids' friends into your family doesn't mean that you can't help your kids draw boundaries with friends or learn to identify safe people and safe friendships. That's critically important, and their friends spending time in your home will help you navigate those relationships with them. But as they learn to navigate friendships, you also teach them to create a culture of blessing as they grow up that they will effortlessly reproduce as they go to college and bless their roommates and even when they start families of their own.

For me, a family taking the chance on giving me their blessing ultimately led me to Christ. You never know the impact that you will make on a child who you welcome into the family. And anyway, it's less about what you do and more about creating an atmosphere of blessing and acceptance in your home.

13

Intergenerational Blessing

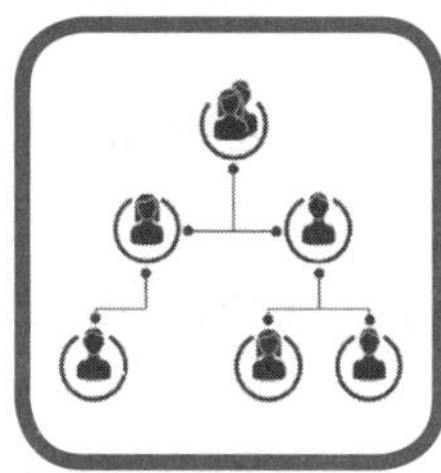

My incredible wife, Cindy, has an amazing heart to serve and love people from all different generations. As a teacher, she works with kids, equipping them with the tools they need to be successful inside and outside of the classroom. But she also has a love for the generations above her as well.

Each Christmas, Cindy would organize a Christmas carol event. She would reach out to a local nursing home and schedule the performance of a kids' singing group at the home. She would then invite families with kids to join us at the nursing home that day.

She would print off several song sheets for everyone in the audience and so the kids singing could look at the words. She brought bells, tambourines, and other musical toys for the kids to play while they sang. She would draft an older kid with piano or guitar experience to lead the group of carolers (after having them prepare and practice the songs for several weeks).

Best of all, all the participants would light up as the men and women in the nursing home warmed up and were filled with joy at the sight of the young kids pouring their hearts out in song.

After the carols, we would have a time to socialize with the residents of the home. The kids would sit on their laps, tell stories, and love on a generation that needed encouragement. Some of those folks didn't have any family left. For others, their family chose not to see them, even at Christmas. They were in deep need of encouragement, hope, laughter, and joy—things kids are able to bring naturally that the rest of us have to work at.

Let me tell you: the five years we did this, there wasn't a dry eye in the place by the time we left (even though I'm still partially claiming my tears were due to allergies). These are some of our favorite holiday memories.

It blessed our kids as well. We began to notice that they would want to talk to older people at the grocery store or stop to help them if they looked like they were in need. Our girls were no longer afraid to talk to adults of any age; they saw that they were people who needed connection and were excited to pour love out to them.

Cindy would also plan a dessert-and-hot-chocolate celebration for the kids and their families at our house after the performance. Everyone would gather together (the younger kids would go play), and we would find ourselves laughing (and sometimes crying) as we shared about the people we connected with that night.

Mom, you can help your kids connect in the same way. It's amazing to see what the blessing from a child can do for someone. It's also amazing to see how the person receiving the blessing can speak over your kids words of life that carry weight due to the wisdom and experience attached to them.

While singing carols at a nursing home is just one way to reach out to older generations, there are tons of other ways that you can help your kids bless and be blessed by different generations:

- Have your kids spend some time reading stories to those in a nursing home.

- If your kids are artistic, have them draw an original picture or make a card for the people they meet at a nursing home.
- Look for opportunities at church, the grocery store, community events, etc. to help your kids build connections, bless, and be blessed by those of all different ages.

Strengths Blessing

As a mom, you get a firsthand look at how unique your kids are. As a parent, you are able to see these qualities as strengths when they are used well and as potential hindrances for your kids when they are used poorly. That's why taking time to affirm and value your kids' strengths is so critical.

Our oldest daughter, Kari, is outgoing, funny, spontaneous, driven, and a kind but passionate leader. It's no wonder that she became a varsity cheerleader, YoungLife leader, and now runs her own company.

Our younger daughter, Laura, is deeply loving, loyal, and kind and has an ability to deeply connect with those who are hurting. She is now a nurse for a free health-care clinic for the uninsured and underinsured. Her goal is to eventually go into full-time missions with nursing.

For our girls, the ability to see these qualities as strengths and to learn to use them well instead of be controlled by them started when they were young. Kari's natural excitement, drive, and spontaneity could sometimes lead her into trouble. Laura's desire to love others and open her kind heart could sometimes lead her to be walked on by those around her.

Mom, it's critical that you see your children's strengths and help them develop them.

For example, for Kari, we were intentional about helping guide her drive. She needed healthy outlets for her energy and a space at home to lead, and we had conversations with her about how she could combine her leadership skills with kindness and planning so that she didn't walk over others and her ideas would have a platform to succeed. We didn't tell her she was wrong to be driven or excited. That was who God created her to be. Cindy and I chose to see those strengths and walk with Kari as she grew into them and into the calling God had for her life.

Mom, you can do the same thing for your kids as well.

If you aren't sure what your children's specific strengths are, I have a helpful tool to help you discover their unique gifts. Included here is the LOGB® Personal Strengths Assessment (That's short for Lion/Otter/Golden Retriever/Beaver!) I created years ago. This is basically a quick quiz to help you determine your God-given strengths and those of each of your children as well. Here's how it works.

First, make a copy of the assessment for yourself and for each child. Starting with the L box, circle every word or phrase that describes you as a person and circle the sentence "Let's do it now!" Consider how you behave overall, rather than just as a mother at home. Are you generally assertive? Circle it. Do you tend to take charge? Circle it. After you've worked through the L box, then do the same in the O box, the G box, and the B box.

L

Takes charge	Bold
Determined	Purposeful
Assertive	Decision maker
Firm	Leader
Enterprising	Goal-driven
Competitive	Self-reliant
Enjoys challenges	Adventurous

"Let's do it now!"

Double the number circled _______

O

Takes risks	Fun-loving
Visionary	Likes variety
Motivator	Enjoys change
Energetic	Creative
Very verbal	Group-oriented
Promoter	Mixes easily
Avoids details	Optimistic

"Trust me! It'll work out!"

Double the number circled _______

G

Loyal	Adaptable
Nondemanding	Sympathetic
Even keel	Thoughtful
Avoids conflict	Nurturing
Enjoys routine	Patient
Dislikes change	Tolerant
Deep relationships	Good listener

"Let's keep things the way they are."

Double the number circled _______

B

Deliberate	Discerning
Controlled	Detailed
Reserved	Analytical
Predictable	Inquisitive
Practical	Precise
Orderly	Persistent
Factual	Scheduled

"How was it done in the past?"

Double the number circled _______

STRENGTHS ASSESSMENT CHART

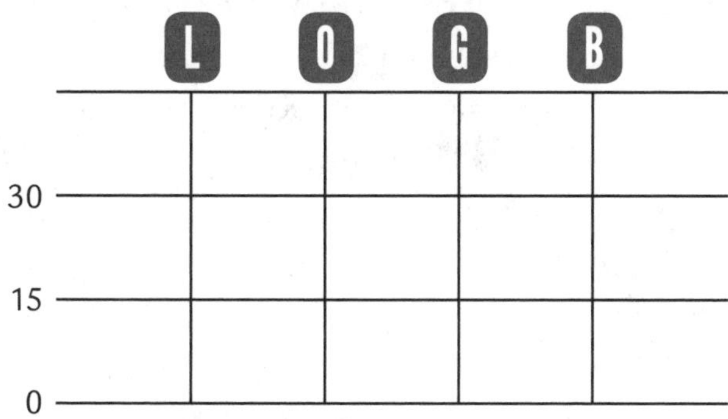

Example:

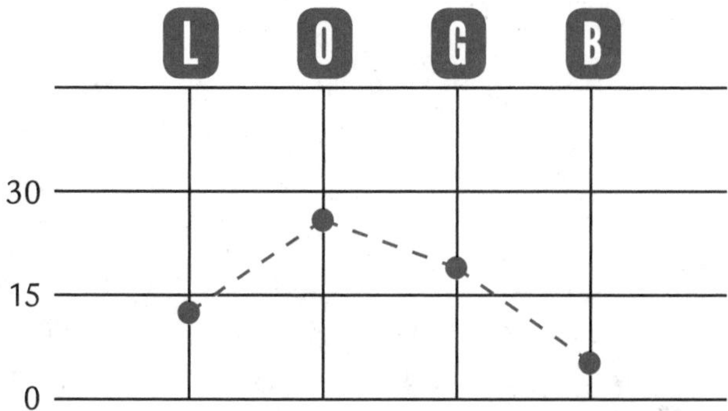

Now you're ready to score your quiz. Start with the L box. At the bottom of the box is a place for the total score. So in the L box, count up all the words and phrases you circled and include the circled sentence at the bottom of the box. Let's say you circled 6 words and/or phrases and the "Let's do it now!" for a total of 7 circles. Now double your score, which would be 14 (that's 7 x 2 = 14). Put 14 where the total score is to go. Go on through the O, G, and B boxes, counting up all the circles and doubling that number for the total score in each. Let's say your total scores were 14 in L, 26 in O, 18 in G, and 4 in B. Take those total scores and mark the appropriate spots on the Strengths Assessment Chart. So on the L line, you'd mark 14; on the O, you'd put a mark roughly where 26 would be, etc. Now connect the dots. What you'll have is a visual graph of your unique, God-given strengths.

After you've taken your assessment, have each of your children take the quiz to figure out their strengths. Depending on their age, you can help with the vocabulary of course, but as much as possible, let them do their own work. When they've finished, double the number of circles in each box, and plot the total scores on the graph. You'll get to see their graph, and this knowledge of how they view themselves—what their God-given strengths are—can be a great tool in blessing your children!

As you'll see, the graph and what it says about each of your children will give you a means of affirming your children by highlighting the strengths you see in them, and you will have a better picture of how they see you.

My friend Gary Smalley and I wrote an entire book about this assessment called *The Two Sides of Love*, but let me give you a snapshot of what L, O, G, and B each look like.

If the highest score on the assessment is in the L box, then you are a Lion. Lions tend to be charge-ahead, take-charge people. They are often the boss (or they think they are). They're good at making quick decisions and can become impatient with anything that gets in their way (like red lights!). They're great leaders who get things done but may need to be better listeners—particularly if their G-box scores are very low.

If you scored highest in the O box, then you are an Otter. Otters are what we call "parties waiting to happen!" They are fun-loving and very verbal, and they usually know hundreds of people—they just don't remember everyone's name! They're great at starting things and creating new things, but they tend not to be thoroughly organized; for example, they can start to balance the checkbook but not finish the task. (And in some cases, they just switch banks to find out their balance!) Otters are the ones with a sock room rather than a meticulously kept sock drawer. They're a lot of fun, but sometimes they need to be more serious or organized to get things done.

Those with the highest G-box scores are Golden Retrievers. They are team players, very consistent, warm, and fuzzy; and they want everyone to feel part of the family. They can often have trouble saying *no*, because they don't want to disappoint anyone. For example, Golden Retrievers tend to buy eighteen to twenty boxes of Girl Scout cookies every year, because it's almost genetically impossible for a Golden Retriever to say one small but very important word: "No!" Despite this, they're great listeners, counselors, and encouragers. But sometimes, they are so soft on people that they can be too soft on problems as well. They have a tendency to struggle with discipline and often push off a problem ("Oh, it'll go away").

Finally, guess what's on the class ring at MIT. Or

at Cal Tech. (Two of our finest engineering schools in the country). Well, if your score is highest in the B box, then you are a Beaver, just like at MIT or Cal Tech! Beavers are organized, detailed, and precise. They like to finish things they start (Otters like to start things and start more things and start more things). Beavers enjoy systems of accomplishing things and are great at detailed work. Because of their attention to even the smallest things, they may be critical of others and can be really hard on themselves. And they often want the string with the ball on the end to be hanging from the ceiling in the garage, because the car needs to go right . . . there!

Once you and your children have completed your assessments, take some time to discuss the results. Who are the Lions in your family? The Otters? The Golden Retrievers? The Beavers? Talk with your children about how they see themselves and how you see them. Talk about how you see yourself and how they see you.

It may be that you see each other very differently than you see yourselves. Give your kids examples of the times you see them act certain ways and let them give you examples of your behavior as well.

Do your best to focus on the strengths, rather than the weaknesses, but you certainly can make plans for how you can work to better understand and encourage one another. Seeing each other's strengths is a powerful means of blessing. It's a way to both attach high value and picture a special future for each child as you encourage them with how you see God using their personality and how you envision he will use it in the future.

While there will probably be one of the personality profiles that you feel most strongly fits each of your children (or yourself), it is important to note that everyone has a blend of the personalities, so some traits of each profile may fit each child. Taking time to be a student of each of your children and learning more about them is crucial to being able to bless them according to their personality (plus, as children are growing, their personalities may take dramatic turns!).

It's sometimes hard to remember that our kids aren't us. They are unique. And our job is to foster the unique talents and gifts that God gave them and help them learn to walk those out in healthy ways that bless others around them.

15

Throw-and-Catch Blessing

One of the best things my mom did to bless me was teach me how to build genuine connection with others.

As an arthritic, my mother couldn't play catch with my brothers and me, but she could have conversations with us. She would ask us a question and then wait patiently for us to answer. It was then our turn to ask her a question. We would do this on road trips, at the dinner table—wherever we were. It took me years to realize that she was teaching each of us to place value on what others had to say, instead of making every conversation all about ourselves.

Mom, there are some very practical ways that you can incorporate in your children's life this way of blessing others.

Cindy and I started with a simple game of catch. We would take a baseball, tennis ball, foam ball, football, Frisbee—really whatever we had lying around the house—and get the girls to join us outside or at a park for a game of catch. While we were tossing the ball back and forth, we added another component to the game: the person holding the ball was not only responsible for throwing it, but that person also had to ask a question of the person they were throwing the ball to. The person catching the ball would answer the question and then ask a question of the person they chose to throw the ball to. The only rule to the game was that no one-word answers were allowed. Let me give you an example:

> Kari, throwing the ball to Laura: "What is your favorite animal?"
>
> Laura, catching the ball: "A monkey!"

If Laura didn't elaborate on that answer, Cindy and I would simply ask why or what questions to help her share more specifics about what she loved about monkeys. This sounds silly, but it teaches your kids to share their heart, instead of just facts. It also teaches them that deep connection and relationship takes communication and understanding the heart behind the answer. Now let me continue the example:

John and Cindy to Laura: "That's great! What is your favorite thing about monkeys? Why do you think they like bananas? If you had a pet monkey, what would you name him?"

After she answered our questions, Laura would then get to throw the ball and ask a question of her choice.

The questions don't have to lead to profound answers, but they should encourage your children to share a little more of their heart behind their answer. The questions during our games ranged from silly to serious, but the takeaway for our girls was huge. We were modeling for them what showing genuine interest in others looked like and giving them practical tools to be able to communicate that in relationships.

Here are some other ways that you can play catch to create blessing:

- Keep a foam ball in the backseat of the car. As Cindy and I sat in the front seat, Kari and Laura would toss a foam back and forth to each other and ask questions until they ran out. Our backseat was full of laughter and joy as our girls were able to get to know each other better and interact in a fun way. Sometimes just sitting down and having a conversation can be intimidating. But adding a tangible activity to it takes the pressure off and allows kids to relax, have fun, and open up. By the way, things kids learn while having fun also stick with them for the long term. We remember positive experiences and the things associated with them. By making genuine connection with others a positive experience, you help them gain an invaluable skill that will stay with them the rest of their lives.

- Keep a ball or Frisbee in the trunk of your car. When you are driving around with your children, stop at a park for ten minutes and play an impromptu game of Catch and Questions. Mom, your children will love having your undivided attention and will think you are the coolest for deciding to spend spontaneous time with them. Another blessing from this is that it allows you to ask deep questions with your kids in a nonthreatening way. I'd start your first few throws with some simple questions, but a relaxed game of catch allows you to address things that may seem hard to talk about if you were sitting across the table and staring at each other. Activity has a way of disarming us and providing a level of comfort that encourages us to share our hearts.

The book of Proverbs tells us that "bright eyes gladden the heart" (Proverbs 15:30). Light up your eyes as your kids share with you. Let them see that you value what's in their minds and hearts—even the silly things. This time intentionally spent with them will not only give them your blessing but also create a trust and openness for them so that they will come to you with real-life situations as they grow up.

Journal Blessing

Being a mother, especially to very young children, can be exceedingly busy. Mothers often say, "Enjoy them while they are young. They grow up so fast." And while this is true, one of the parts of enjoying them is making an effort to remember some of the sweet details of their life. A lot of young mothers these days use Facebook to catalog the hilarious, tender, and even embarrassing moments of their children's lives, and I think this is excellent! I would encourage you to write down or type out the little moments that otherwise would likely get lost as years go by. Write down that your child says "muh-rote" for "remote" or that they wrinkle their nose and sniff whenever they hear a dog. Write down when your child takes their first steps and when they make their first basketball goal and when they tell you they can walk to their new classroom by themselves. Choosing to record these things as they happen will give you a tool that you can use to encourage your children as you watch them grow. Capture the moments in writing!

Snack-and-Chat Blessing

If you're home when your son or daughter gets home from school, make a habit of having a snack with them and chatting with them about their day. The conversation can start with something as simple as "What was the best part of your day?" Then follow up with "What was the worst part?" Creating with your children a routine of expressing interest in their lives is a great way to connect with them and foster a positive relationship of acceptance. Let your kids know that you care and genuinely want to know about the great and not-so-great parts of their lives and that they can feel safe sharing these things with you.

18

Fresh-Air Blessing

There has been increased emphasis on getting kids to engage in active play as technology lures them to remain stationary and inside. While there are appropriate times for technology, make sure that your kids have boundaries established for playing video games or using the computer. Unfortunately, the epidemic of people cooped up inside with their techie devices isn't limited to children–adults are perhaps even more guilty! Make an effort to be outside with your kids, not only as an observer, but also as an active participant. Take a break from your TV, laptop, and cell phone and give your kids undivided attention while you're outside.

One tradition that our family has is to take a hike each year on Thanksgiving Day (weather permitting). There is something about being outside in nature together that brings an awareness of the majesty of God and the rich blessings he pours out on our lives. Some years our hikes are more leisurely than others, but putting in a little bit of work helps us earn our turkey dinner, and our girls look forward to the time that we spend together on our hikes. Cindy champions getting everyone out the door and making sure the hike happens, as she believes the time taken to connect with our girls is valuable. As often as you can, be outside with your children and connect in ways that aren't cluttered by technology.

Mommy-Date Blessing

I think a great practice is having a date once a month with each of your children. A lot of times moms are so busy taking care of the physical wellbeing of all members of the family that spending quality one-on-one time with family members has to be done very intentionally. A great way to do this is by going on a date with each member of the family on the day of the month that is the same as their birthday—in other words, if their birthday is September 12, you would go on a date on the twelfth of each month. The date doesn't have to be complicated. It could simply be a walk around the neighborhood! But setting aside time each month to spend with just your son or daughter is a great way to bless your child and demonstrate to them your active commitment to them. Each month on your date, celebrate your child by spending some special one-on-one time with him or her.

Family-and-Friends Blessing

Passing on the blessing to your children should include the encouragement of your children from those who have positive relationships with them. One way to do this is to invite family members and friends to share in written notes a special memory or something they appreciate about your child. You might give these to your child on a special occasion or just as a surprise. Be sure to write a note yourself to include with the others and let your child know that they matter. I know one young mother who has already established a tradition of having birthday party guests write blessings each year for her child. A written blessing can be as simple as "I'm praying for you to show others how brave you are this year!" or "I am so proud of how creative and kind you are!" Inviting others to bless your children lets them know that they have a team in their corner; this in turn can unleash your children to pursue their potential perhaps more than anything else.

Chore Blessing

Recently a mother joked to me that she needed to have more kids so that she would have more help with housework. Ha! I suppose the adage "Many hands make light work" can ring true when it comes to household chores once those hands reach a certain size, but it certainly isn't an instant thing! Involving your children in doing chores is important in teaching them responsibility and discipline, and children can learn a sense of pride as they learn to take care of their things and their home.

It often seems, though, that there is at least one chore that children struggle with more than others. For our daughter Laura, it was making her bed. It always seemed that making her bed was avoided until the last minute, and she just struggled to do the task well. One morning, I noticed that her bed was still not made and we needed to be leaving for school soon. I walked into her room, grabbed the sheet on one side of the bed, and said, "Laura, could you help me with this?" She quickly caught on to what I was doing, grabbed the sheet on the opposite side of the bed, and worked with me until all of the linens and pillows were in place. I could have fussed at Laura for not completing the task, but instead, I chose to bless her by helping her complete the task.

I'm not saying to let your children off the hook from doing their chores, but choosing to help them with a particular task that they struggle with can be a real way to bless them and show them that you care.

22

Ready-for-Worship Blessing

There is wisdom in the words "Sunday church begins Saturday night." For those who are part of making the church service happen, preparation starts long before Saturday arrives! But helping your children to prepare for church on Saturday night will help all those in your home be able to celebrate going to worship together. Teaching your kids that corporate worship is a joyous occasion is invaluable. Sunday mornings in the home can often be hectic, and getting out the door can be frustrating and put everyone in foul moods. To prevent this, help your children Saturday night prepare in practical ways for worship by choosing clothes for the morning, gathering items that will be taken (Bible, pen, journal, offering, etc.), and praying together for God to prepare your hearts to hear from him as you gather with other believers. Teaching your children that going to church is one of the ways that we worship God is a priceless lesson.

23

Rest Blessing

We live in a very busy world. Constant activity. Constant options. Instant gratification. Persistent impatience. Everything is faster than it's ever been, but it's still not fast enough. There is a great temptation to involve our kids in every sport and activity—we want them to be well rounded, right? But I want to encourage you to build margin into your family life and bless your children by teaching them that rest is important. Cindy has always done a great job of protecting our family time and encouraging us to rest, particularly in regard to the Sabbath, which is about stepping away from work and activity to hear the Lord.

In seeking to create a culture of blessing within your home, make an effort to protect your children from the lure of overscheduling. Help them to make choices about what they will be involved in and to be genuinely invested in what they choose, rather than minimally invested in a large array of activities. This doesn't mean you shouldn't encourage your kids to try different things and discover how they are gifted, but they don't have to do every available activity at the same time!

Have at least one night a week that is protected as family night, a night on which everyone is expected to be home and maybe even to go to bed early! Establish boundaries for your family and make sure there is margin in your family life so that you can each take time to reflect on what God is doing and rest in him. As Psalm 63:1 reminds us: "O God, you are my God; earnestly I seek you; my soul thirsts for you; my flesh faints for you, as in a dry and weary land where there is no water" (ESV).

24

Scripture-Memory Blessing

Hear, O Israel:
The LORD our God, the LORD is one.
You shall love the LORD your God
with all your heart and with all your soul
and with all your might.
And these words that I command you today
shall be on your heart.
You shall teach them diligently to your
children, and shall talk of them
when you sit in your house,
and when you walk by the way,
and when you lie down, and when you rise.
You shall bind them as a sign on your hand,
and they shall be as frontlets
between your eyes.
You shall write them on the doorposts of
your house and on your gates.

[Deuteronomy 6:4-9, ESV]

Jewish households took these words spoken by Moses literally. The doorposts of homes were engraved with Scripture, and Jewish men would bind to their arms small leather boxes containing pieces of parchment paper with the verses written on them. Aside from the literal interpretation of these verses from Deuteronomy, these verses can also be interpreted to mean that a reverence for God's Word should be experienced within the gates and beyond the doors of the home, that the works of the hands and viewings of the eyes should be filtered through what is honoring to the commands of the Lord. Does your family approach Scripture this way?

I would encourage you to start small with your children and choose to memorize one verse together each month. Review the verse regularly. Talk about any times when God has brought the verse to mind throughout your day. Ask your children if the meaning of the verse has changed at all for them over time. Teaching your children to know and love God's Word is a powerful way to bless them. You might start by memorizing a verse of blessing for your children! Let them know that you are praying that verse for them. Jeremiah 29:11 is always a great verse to start with.

"For I know the plans I have for you," declares the LORD,
"plans to prosper you and not to harm you,
plans to give you hope and a future."
Jeremiah 29:11, NIV

With whatever verse you begin, making a habit of memorizing God's Word together can make a world of difference in establishing a culture of blessing within your home.

Verses to Memorize With Younger Children

Be kind to one another, tenderhearted, forgiving one another, as God in Christ forgave you.
Ephesians 4:32

When I am afraid, I put my trust in you.
Psalm 56:3

The LORD is good to all,
and his mercy is over all that he has made.
Psalm 145:9

Children, obey your parents in the Lord, for this is right.
Ephesians 6:1

You shall love the LORD your God with all your heart and with all your soul and with all your might.
Deuteronomy 6:5

Trust in the LORD with all your heart,
and do not lean on your own understanding.
Proverbs 3:5

Let everything that has breath praise the LORD!
Praise the LORD!
Psalm 150:6

We love because he first loved us.
1 John 4:19

Rejoice in the Lord always; again I will say, rejoice.
Philippians 4:4

Verses to Memorize With Older Children

But may all who seek you rejoice and be glad in you;
may those who love your salvation say continually,
"Great is the LORD!"
Psalm 40:16

The heavens declare the glory of God,
and the sky above proclaims his handiwork.
Psalm 19:1

For great is the LORD, *and greatly to be praised;*
he is to be feared above all gods.
Psalm 96:4

Let no corrupting talk come out of your mouths, but only such as is good for building up, as fits the occasion, that it may give grace to those who hear.
Ephesians 4:29

For I delivered to you as of first importance what I also received: that Christ died for our sins in accordance with the Scriptures, that he was buried, that he was raised on the third day in accordance with the Scriptures.
1 Corinthians 15:3-4

Finally, brothers, whatever is true, whatever is honorable, whatever is just, whatever is pure, whatever is lovely, whatever is commendable, if there is any excellence, if there is anything worthy of praise, think about these things.
Philippians 4:8

25

Looking-Forward Blessing

One of the most unique elements of the giving of the blessing is picturing a special future for your child. As you become a student of each of your children and you see them grow into their strengths, you can encourage them to think about what God has in store for them in the future. The question, "What do you want to be when you grow up?" can't come too early! Encourage your children to think about what they want to pursue in life and how they can use their gifts for God's glory. Dream with them about what career they might pursue, what kind of person they might marry, how many children of their own they might have one day. Help them see how their actions today impact their future, and encourage them to take that into account when they make choices.

26

Thank-You Blessings

I know one mother who is really great at blessing her kids by teaching them to write thank-you notes. While sometimes thank-you notes can be shallow and simply say "Thanks for the gift!" this mother encourages her children to write notes that go beyond thanking someone for a physical item and to thank that person for their friendship, character, example, etc. Her daughter took the teaching to heart and said to me, "If I'm going to go to the trouble to write a card, I want to fill it with meaningful words, not just a polite thank-you." Teaching your children to make a habit of thanking others for gifts or special acts of care can go a long way, and teaching them to go above and beyond in thanking a person through a thoughtful note is a great way to challenge your children to bless others.

27

Own-Your-Mistakes Blessing

Parenting takes you through a progression of stages as each of your children grows and matures. I would encourage you to start early in making a habit of apologizing to your children when you mess up. Being authentic with your children shows them that you value them, that it matters to you when you don't treat them or others in the best possible way, that you want to be all you can be and set an example for them so that they can be all they can be. I've heard some people say that their mother taught them to never say "I'm sorry," because that could mean "I am a sorry person," but instead to say "I apologize." While I think the words "I'm sorry" are acceptable, this is an interesting perspective as it reminds us that even when we mess up, we are loved unconditionally by our Creator, and we don't lose his blessing because of our mistakes. Modeling this for your children and starting as early as you can will bless them immensely.

28

Creative-Prayer Blessing

I cannot emphasize enough the value of praying for and praying with your children. There are plenty of creative ways to pray with them. Here are a few suggestions:

- Get a chalkboard to hang up at the dinner table. Every night at dinner, ask each person to list one thing they could use prayer about for the following day, and write it on the board. Pray about the requests together as a family. The next night at dinner, go down the prayer list and let each person provide an update on the outcome. Celebrate the successes and mourn the losses together as a family. Then come together to add new items for the next day. This is a great way to keep track of daily achievements and victories together.

- ➲ Make a prayer calendar with your kids for the whole year. Talk about things you can pray about each month and on specific days throughout the year and write reminders on the calendar. You can add things to the calendar at any time, and each day take a few minutes to pray with your son or daughter about the items on the calendar.
- ➲ Practice praying out loud with your son or daughter as you go through your daily routine. If your children are anxious about something, stop and pray a short sentence prayer with them that God will calm their heart and give them peace. If they experience disappointment with a friend, stop and pray about the situation. If they are having trouble choosing between great opportunities that have presented themselves, take a moment to pray with them for wisdom. Praying with and for your children doesn't have to be complicated. It's all about acknowledging that God is present with us at all times and cares about every detail of our lives.

With good reason, Paul told us: "Rejoice always, pray without ceasing, give thanks in all circumstances; for this is the will of God in Christ Jesus for you" (1 Thessalonians 5:16-18, ESV).

29

Serving Blessing

As you strive to give your children the blessing, I encourage you to bless them by teaching them to serve. Jesus was the ultimate example to us of a servant leader. He taught his followers that even he, the King of kings, "did not come to be served, but to serve" (Matthew 20:28, NIV). As you discover more about the ways that your children are gifted and what their strengths are, look for opportunities for them to use those strengths for the benefit of others. Find ways to volunteer as a family—through church, a local nonprofit, a soup kitchen, a missions trip, etc. Teach your kids that investing in others around them not only blesses the person they are helping, but creates blessing for them as well.

Help your kids find a cause that they are passionate about, and help them get involved in it. It may be special-needs kids, animals, orphans in Zambia, or even a local nonprofit. Whatever it is that gets them excited and blesses others, encourage them to find a way to give time, money, and prayers to support that cause.

Jim Elliot was a missionary who gave his life in seeking to share the gospel with others. He said something before he died that is so true: "He is no fool who gives up what he cannot keep to gain what he cannot lose." You can't out-give God, and your giving to others will be a blessing to you and to your children.

30

Rite-of-Passage Blessing

We have reached the final of our thirty ideas for blessing your children. And this is a big one. I would encourage you to acknowledge certain turning points in your children's life and take the time to give them a special rite-of-passage blessing. Maybe that will be when they put their faith in Christ, are baptized, enter middle school, get their driver's license, or graduate from high school. These times are pivotal in your children's life, and reassuring them with a written and spoken blessing during these times is of great value. As you create an everyday culture of blessing within your home, don't miss out on giving unique and special blessings to each of your children for the *big* moments of their life either. Celebrate those turning points and make a big deal about blessing your children in those once-in-a-lifetime moments.

LET THE BLESSING BEGIN

Mom, you have an amazing job. You get to influence the next generation in a way that is more powerful than anyone else. I pray that you are encouraged along your journey as a mother. I hope that you know that you are loved infinitely by your Father in heaven who is faithful to equip you for every good work. You can impact your children and give them the blessing. The Lord is with you. Make the most of every opportunity.

I'm praying for you as you embark on this journey to bless your children. Keep your eyes fixed on the Lord. Seek him earnestly and he will honor you as you seek to bless your family. May you carry this prayer with you as you create the habit of blessing your children:

May the Lord bless you and keep you.
May he make his face to shine on you,
and be gracious to you. May he lift up his
countenance on you and give you peace

[Numbers 6:24-26].

Father God,

Thank you for the mother who is reading this and who desires to bless her children.

Lord, I pray that she herself experienced the blessing.

I pray Lord, that she knows what it means to be touched in a way that expresses care, tenderness, and strength.

I pray that she has heard words
spoken to her that communicate
that she is of great worth, that you have
created her uniquely, and that you have
remarkable plans for her.

I sincerely hope that she has received the
blessing from her own mother, but, Lord,
if she didn't, I pray that she will embrace
the blessing that you bestow upon her.

As she strives to then bless
her sons and daughters,
may those young men and women that
you have placed in her care grow to be a
generation who loves you deeply and serves
you with a passion as they know
that they were created for a purpose.

We love you, Lord Jesus,
and trust you to do beyond
what we could ever ask or imagine.

In your Son's precious name we do pray.
Amen.

Bring the Blessing to Your Home

A spouse's or a parent's approval affects the way people view themselves. You can give your spouse and/or your children the gift of unconditional acceptance the Bible calls the blessing. This set of four short booklets is packed with tips on what the blessing is, and each booklet gives 30 ideas on how to give it to those around you. Even if you didn't get the blessing as a child, you can learn to give it to others.

Author John Trent is a Christian psychologist and co-author of the million-copy bestselling book, *The Blessing*. He shares his own story of his father's abandonment, and how he learned to give the blessing to his children.

Paperback, 112 pages, 4.5 x 6.5 x .25 inches

30 Ways a Father Can Bless His Children
9781628622775 4077X

30 Ways a Mother Can Bless Her Children
9781628622805 4078X

30 Ways a Husband Can Bless His Wife
9781628622836 4079X

30 Ways a Wife Can Bless Her Husband
9781628622867 4080X